Who Is
Nathan Chen?

Who Is
Nathan Chen?

by Joseph Liu

illustrated by Gregory Copeland

Penguin Workshop

PENGUIN WORKSHOP
An imprint of Penguin Random House LLC, New York

First published in the United States of America by Penguin Workshop,
an imprint of Penguin Random House LLC, New York, 2023

Visit us online at penguinrandomhouse.com.

Library of Congress Control Number: 2023013432

Printed in the United States of America

ISBN 9780593661000 (paperback)   10 9 8 7 6 5 4 3 2 1 WOR
ISBN 9780593661017 (library binding)   10 9 8 7 6 5 4 3 2 1 WOR

Contents

Who Is Nathan Chen?

During the 2022 Winter Olympics, Nathan Chen stood alone in the middle of the ice rink in Beijing (say: BAY-jing), China. His legs were spread apart and his arms were relaxed at his side. He was dressed in black pants and a red shirt covered in stars. The stars were not like those you see on a flag. These were more like stars you see in space. They shone brightly on his red shirt, just like he did against the white ice.

Softly, music started playing in the Capital Indoor Stadium. Nathan closed his eyes, raised his right hand, and spun. He glided across the ice, skating and dancing along with the music. The song was "Rocket Man" by Elton John. It is about an astronaut that is leaving Earth. Nathan's star-covered shirt matched the song perfectly.

Suddenly, he leaped into the air. With his arms crossed tightly against his chest, he spun. He went around one, two, three, four times. The music spiked and crashed right as he landed back on the ice. His skates barely touched the ground before he was in the air again. This time he spun two times and landed safely on his feet.

The crowd cheered as the music picked up speed, and Nathan danced and glided around on the ice.

These jumps with four spins are called quadruple jumps, also known as quads. Nathan performed four more quads before his routine was over. He is the first person ever to do five different quads in a single performance! These spinning jumps are the reason why he is known as the "Quad King."

After four and a half minutes of incredible skating, Nathan's routine finished. The crowd was on its feet, and Nathan knew he'd done an amazing job.

Sitting in the booth, Nathan waited for the judges to report his scores. The seconds ticked by while everyone waited in silence. After what seemed like a lifetime, his scores appeared. The crowd roared and Nathan clasped his hands to his head. He had won the gold medal. He was now an Olympic champion. Even though he was wearing a mask because of the coronavirus pandemic, everyone could see he was smiling.

Nathan wins the Olympic gold medal, 2022.

CHAPTER 1
Born into a Family of Skaters

On May 5, 1999, Zhidong Chen and his wife Hetty Wang welcomed a newborn son they named Nathan. They had left China and lived in Salt Lake City, Utah, with their four other children, two boys and two girls. All four of those children were skaters, and baby Nathan would be, too.

Nathan's older brothers are named Tony and Colin. He grew up watching them play ice hockey. Each weekend Nathan would watch his brothers score goals and battle for the puck. His older sisters are named Alice and Janice. They also skated. They didn't play hockey though; they figure-skated. Figure skating is dancing on ice, where skaters spin and jump to music. In competitions, they are scored based on how well they perform their routines.

When Nathan was just three years old, Salt Lake City hosted the Winter Olympics. At this very young age, Nathan had the wonderful opportunity to see world famous athletes, like Michelle Kwan, compete in his hometown.

Michelle Kwan is a Chinese American skater who had won silver at the 1998 Winter Olympics and then bronze during the 2002 Olympics in Salt Lake City. (She has also won the US Championships nine times and the

World Championships five times.)

Nathan looked up to Michelle Kwan and her many skating victories. After seeing her compete at the 2002 Olympics, Nathan learned about another Asian American skater, Kristi Yamaguchi. Kristi, a Japanese American skater, had won the gold medal at the 1992 Winter Olympics. She also won the US Championships twice and World Championships once. These two Asian American women inspired Nathan to believe he could be great. They are among the reasons he started skating. Seeing people who looked like him becoming so successful on the ice gave Nathan the drive to begin skating at age three.

Growing up, Nathan's family didn't have much money. When he started figure skating, he used the same pair of skates that he did when he played hockey. However, hockey skates have curved blades and make it easier to fall backward.

His mom bought him his first pair of figure skates. She picked out a white pair for him, since the white ones were cheaper than the black ones. What his mom didn't know was that white skates were worn by girls and black ones were worn by boys. People thought these skates were his sister's old hand-me-downs.

As Nathan grew, he quickly became too big for these white skates. He needed a new pair, but his family did not have enough money to buy them for him.

His dad thought he might have a solution. He had heard about a place that gave money to help people who wanted to skate, called the Michael Weiss Foundation. It was created by Michael Weiss, a figure skater who had gone to the Olympics twice and had been the US National Champion three times.

Nathan's dad applied for a scholarship to help pay for Nathan's skates. There was just one problem: Nathan was only ten, too young for the scholarship. News about how much Nathan wanted to skate started spreading around the foundation. It eventually made it to Michael

Weiss himself. When he heard about Nathan, he knew that he wanted to help even if Nathan was too young for the scholarship. He gave the family $200, and Nathan was able to get a brand-new pair of skates in his new size.

Those skates meant the world to Nathan. Now he could keep skating and work toward his dreams. Michael's generosity had kickstarted Nathan's career.

At age seven, Nathan started ballet lessons at the Ballet West Academy. He became a talented dancer, performing in ballets such as *The Nutcracker*, *Swan Lake*, and *Sleeping Beauty*. Learning how to dance on stage helped him become a fantastic dancer on ice. Not only did it teach him how to move to music beautifully, it also taught him how to not get nervous when performing in front of people.

CHAPTER 2
Driving for a Dream

In 2003, when Nathan was four years old, he began competitive figure skating. He started small, at local and regional competitions. By 2007, he had won enough competitions to land a spot at the US Junior Nationals. He would compete against young skaters from all over the United States. That first year, he won tenth place. Just two years later, in 2009, he took home second place and the silver medal. His second-place finish earned him a spot at that season's US Championships.

The US Championships has different levels. This is so that skaters compete against other skaters around their same skill level. That year, Nathan entered the US Championships at the novice level, the third hardest. Junior level is the second hardest and senior level is the hardest.

At the 2010 US Championships, Nathan skated to *Peter and the Wolf*, a musical story about a boy who outsmarts a wolf with the help of his animal friends. In this song, there are

many different instruments. There are violins, cellos, trumpets, and horns. Each instrument represents an animal. Just as the characters create the drama, the instruments all work together to create the music.

At just ten years old, Nathan won the 2010 US Championships and made history as the youngest novice champion ever!

In January of 2011, Nathan held on to his champion title, winning the novice US Championships again.

Nathan was a rising star, and he needed a great coach to help him get even better. Since his family didn't have much money, his mom, Hetty, was his first coach. From his first shaky steps on the ice to the US Championships, she coached him on how to be a better figure skater. Now that he was competing at a national level, he needed a professional coach. His family heard of an amazing coach who specialized in jumps named Rafael Arutunian. However, Rafael lived many miles away in California. Nathan's family lived in Utah. What could they do?

Hetty decided that she and Nathan would drive all the way to California for his lessons.

So, in 2011, Hetty and Nathan would pack up the car and drive the ten hours from Salt Lake City, Utah, to Lake Arrowhead, California, multiple times. They would stay for days or weeks at a time so that Nathan could train. It was a long drive in a small car, but the time that Nathan got to spend with his mom meant a lot to him. Although Nathan was now training with Rafael, Hetty continued to play an important role in his skating career, as his coach and as a parent.

In December of 2011, Nathan and Hetty decided that these trips were not enough. If he wanted to keep winning, he needed to start training with his jump coach full-time. That meant that he had to be in California more often. Driving ten hours to train would be too difficult, but his family couldn't leave Utah. The family made the difficult decision that just Nathan and his mother would move to

California. His dad, brothers, and sisters all stayed in Utah.

It was a hard time for Nathan's family, but his training was very important. Hetty worked multiple jobs so they could pay for his lessons and buy him new skates when he needed them. Nathan worked hard. He appreciated his family's sacrifice.

In 2012, he competed in his first junior level championship and won the US junior champion title! His family's sacrifice had paid off. He was twelve years old.

Already making a name for himself in the United States, Nathan was ready to step onto the world scene. In 2012, he competed in the International Skating Union Junior Grand Prix. The ISU Junior Grand Prix has six events that take place in different nations around the world. At the end of the season, there is a final competition.

At his first ISU Junior Grand Prix event in Austria, he not only won, but his score was the highest anyone had ever scored!

CHAPTER 3
The Quad King Earns His Crown

Nathan was winning a lot of competitions, but he knew he had to train harder to make it to the next Olympics. He knew that his dream of winning at the Olympics would not be easy. And Nathan understood that he would be competing against other skaters from around the world, many of whom were older than him and had already learned two or three different quad jumps.

There are several different types of quad jumps. Before he became the Quad King he is known as today, Nathan needed to learn many of the ones used in competition. To properly perform a quad jump, the skater needs to spin four times in the air. Most quad jumps start

with the skater gliding backward and on one
foot. The difference is how the skater jumps and
lands.

The simplest type of quad jump is the loop.
In the loop, the skater jumps from and lands on
the same foot. The toe loop is almost the same as
the loop. In the toe loop, the skater uses the front

of the other skate, also called a toe, to help them jump.

The flip is another type of quad jump. Just like the toe loop, skaters use the other toe to help them jump. For the flip, they land on the other foot instead of the one they jumped off.

The Salchow (say: SAL-kow) doesn't use the

other toe to help them jump, but the skater switches feet. That means you jump from one foot and land on the other foot.

The Lutz is just like the flip, but the skater spins in the opposite direction of where they started. So if they are turning left before they jump, they spin toward the right while in the air.

The Axel is the most difficult quad. The skater jumps off one foot and lands on the other foot. But the Axel is the only quad where the skater starts facing forward. That means they have to spin four and a half times. No skater had ever successfully done a quad Axel in competition until American Ilia Malinin, from Virginia, landed one in September 2022.

In 2015, Nathan won three of the ISU Junior Grand Prix competitions around the world. He even won the ISU Junior Grand Prix final in December!

One month later, he was ready to show his

new quad jumps at the 2016 US Championships. Nathan competed at the senior level, the most difficult. He landed four quad jumps in one performance, the first American ever to do so! Even though his training had paid off and his quad jumps were great, he placed third. The senior level competition is intense.

That competition showed Nathan that skating was not just about jumps. His jumps were impressive, but the judges wanted to see more. The way skaters move to the rhythm of the music and how their movements flow from one to the next are also important. If he wanted to score higher, Nathan's routines would need to be more than quad jumps—he would need to spin and glide. He would need to dance. This was an important lesson to learn as he prepared for the Olympics.

Nathan remained optimistic. For him, placing third at the US Championships was a huge victory. "This is an awesome step for me as a senior skater," he said. Later at that US Championships, however, Nathan would face a major hurdle to his Olympic dreams.

After a competition is over, skaters give a performance for the fans to enjoy that is not judged. It is called the Skating Spectacular. It isn't part of the competition, and skaters can perform for the fans without worrying about scores. During Nathan's Skating Spectacular, he hurt his hip very badly and needed to have surgery. He was sixteen and was growing very fast. He had also been training very hard. Those two things combined to cause an injury where his tendon pulled a piece off of the bone.

It was two months before he could walk without crutches and another month before he could train in a gym. It was a very difficult time for Nathan. He just wanted to get back to his training and live his usual life again.

But it took six months for him to recover and start skating again. His big dream was to win gold at the 2018 Winter Olympics in PyeongChang (say: Pee-YONG-chong), South Korea. And that was just two years away.

CHAPTER 4
Duct-Taped Skates and a Big Mistake

In October 2016, Nathan had healed from his injury and was ready to compete. At his second Grand Prix event at the senior level, he won second place. He was seventeen, and the second-youngest man to win a senior Grand Prix medal ever.

In January 2017, he entered his second senior US Championships, where he had come in third the year before. During his competition, he broke records again by landing five quad jumps and received the highest score in US Championship history ever. He was crowned the US Men's Champion for the first time.

Nathan was on a winning streak and seemed to be well on his way to the Olympics.

In their first step to get into the Olympics, athletes have to earn spots for the country for which they compete. They can earn their places at the Olympics by doing well at certain competitions. In those important competitions, the combined scores of all the athletes from their country determine how many athletes that country can send to the Olympics. One of these competitions is the World Championships.

Nathan competed at his first World Championships later that year. He wanted to do well, especially after his injury. He wasn't just skating for himself; his score would help the United States earn spots at the Olympics. When he stepped onto the ice, though, people could see something was off. His skates were held together with duct tape!

Nathan had been skating with these skates for so long that they were falling apart. He had a pair of new skates, but they were too stiff. Skates need to bend and move. If they are too rigid, the skate won't turn and bend the right way. Nathan couldn't wear his new skates for this competition so he had to use his old, worn-out skates.

In his duct-taped skates, Nathan tried to do six quad jumps. He fell on two of them. The outside of his skate wouldn't let him land certain jumps. He knew he couldn't skate the way he practiced, so he had to adjust his routine while in the middle of skating. Broken skates, a new routine, and the pressure of an important competition all added up. He placed a disappointing sixth at the World Championships.

Nathan understood that all skaters have to deal with the mental and physical pressures of skating. He didn't handle it the right way that day. Nathan was disappointed by his performance, and knew what it felt like to fail. The only thing he could do was to learn from the experience and put it behind him. Nathan now always keeps a few pairs of skates ready that he can wear at competitions.

Even though sixth place was not as good as he wanted, Nathan was still able to get a spot on the

Olympic team. Jason Brown, his US teammate, had come in seventh. Together they earned enough points for them both to have spots at the 2018 Winter Olympics, as well as an extra spot for an additional teammate.

However, the 2018 Winter Olympics in South Korea would not be the victory that Nathan and all his fans had hoped for.

When the 2018 Winter Olympics arrived, Nathan was nervous. At eighteen years old, he was expected to do very well. He had been on the world stage before, but this was the Olympics! He had trained his whole life for this.

In skating competitions, athletes have two performances. The first one is called the short program, and the second is called the long program or free skate. The short program is two minutes and forty seconds long and has a set of moves that skaters are required to do. The free skate gives athletes more time and freedom to perform their routines. It is four and a half minutes long for men (four minutes for women), and skaters can perform any set of moves they choose. The two scores are added together and whoever gets the highest combined score wins.

For his short program, he wore black pants and a shirt that was all black, except for one sleeve which was white. When he moved, it looked like one of his arms would disappear because the ice was also white. He skated to a song called "Nemesis." It is a fast-paced song with a catchy beat. Matching the rhythm of the song, Nathan energetically skated around the rink, even dancing on his toes at one point.

About thirty seconds into his performance, disaster struck. He launched himself into his first quad jump. He quickly spun four times, but he missed the landing and fell! In the blink of an eye, he was back up and skating. He finished his routine, but after the short program, Nathan was in seventeenth place.

Winning a medal was not possible because his score was so low, but for his free skate, he was determined to skate for himself. He overcame his nerves and put his mistakes behind him. He gave it his all and put on an amazing performance.

Nathan dressed in black-and-white again, but instead of a white sleeve on his shirt, a white edge went around his collar and crossed at his chest. He skated to music from *Mao's Last Dancer*, a film about a ballet dancer who leaves China.

Before he began his performance, Nathan had a look of determination on his face. The cello played a deep drawn-out note and Nathan launched into action. In the short program, he had bounced and swung, but in this performance, he moved slowly and smoothly. He nailed his first quad jump and completed four more. He tried for six, but he did not land the third well enough for it to count. Even without that jump, he made Olympic history. He was the first skater to land five quad jumps in one program! His free skate score became the highest in Olympic history. It was a historic day for Nathan.

Unfortunately, when the judges combined his scores, the total earned him fifth place at the 2018 Winter Olympics, not enough for a personal medal. Although he didn't win in his personal event, Nathan didn't leave empty-handed. He and his teammates took home bronze for the United States in the team event, a separate competition that added up all their scores.

His 2018 season wasn't over when the Olympics finished. He wanted to go out with a win. Just one month after getting fifth place at the PyeongChang Olympics in South Korea, he was at the World Championships in Milan, Italy. He was ready to prove to himself, and the world, that he was the best.

He performed the same routine he did in the Olympics, but this time he landed all six of his quad jumps perfectly. He had done it. Nathan had won his first world championship!

Mao's Last Dancer

Mao's Last Dancer is a film that tells the true story of Li Cunxin (say: lee schwin-sing). The title refers to Mao Zedong (say: MOU zeh doong), the leader of the Chinese government at that time.

Li Cunxin

Cunxin was a ballet dancer in China and was invited to train in America. While living in America in 1981, he realized that he didn't want to go back to China. After a lot of stressful negotiating, he was allowed to stay, but he could never return to China. It was many years later that the Chinese government finally allowed his parents to visit him in America. In 2003 Cunxin wrote a book about his experiences, which became a movie in 2009.

Nathan chose to skate to the soundtrack from this movie to honor his parents' journey from China to America. Although not as difficult at Cunxin's, they had faced their own problems. Nathan even spoke to Cunxin before the 2018 Olympics. He told Nathan, "You have devastating defeat and you learn from that and it is going to make your success that much more rewarding."

It wasn't until 2018 that Cunxin was finally allowed to return to China to dance.

CHAPTER 5
A Medal for Mom

Four years after the 2018 Winter Olympics, Nathan was ready to compete for the gold again at the 2022 Winter Olympics in Beijing, China. It had been a very busy four years for Nathan.

In 2018, just a few months after his first Olympics, he had moved away from his family and started college at Yale University in New Haven, Connecticut. Yale is part of what is known as the Ivy League, a group of some of the best colleges in America.

He wanted to study statistics and data science. Statistics involves finding a meaning or pattern in a set of information. It can help you predict the weather, or the reading level of your classmates.

Most athletes do not go to school while they are

still competing since they are very busy. Nathan would need to attend classes, do homework, and study for tests, all while also practicing his skating for many hours each day. He would have to find time to travel around the world to compete. It would not be easy.

Nathan's decision to start college meant that he was preparing for the next chapter of his life, one that would come after he couldn't skate competitively anymore. His injury in 2016 taught him that he would not be able to skate forever. Nathan understood that having an education and a college degree would make his transition from professional skating to a life outside of constant competition easier.

Nathan was not ready to stop yet, though. Between the 2018 and 2022 Winter Olympics, Nathan won all four US Championships and every single World Championship! (The 2020 World Championships was canceled because of the COVID-19 coronavirus pandemic.) He also won eight ISU Grand Prix competitions in a row.

All his victories showed that he had learned a lot since the 2018 Winter Olympics. Losing on the Olympic world stage taught him a lot, and showed him how to bounce back. He had to be okay with losing and choose to learn from his mistakes rather than let them discourage him.

Now, in 2022, he was ready to step onto the ice again. Nathan was different, but so were the Olympics. The pandemic had swept around the world and changed everything. People had to be careful to not spread the very contagious disease. Social distancing and masks were still common. The pandemic also meant that they had new safety rules at the Olympics. Athletes were tested for COVID-19 every day and they had to stay separated. No spectators could travel to the Olympics, so the crowds were also a lot smaller.

For Nathan, this Olympics was important to him, and his family as well. Beijing was where his mother had grown up. To not only win gold, but to do it in Hetty's hometown, would be amazing. He had traveled to Beijing with his family when he was younger and remembered a lot of the places they had visited. He knew that it meant a lot to his mom that he was competing there. He wanted to make her proud, especially after all she had done to help him in his skating career.

When it came time for him to compete, he made history again. In the short program, his first performance, he achieved a world record score. His free skate, the second performance, was to Elton John's "Rocket Man" and he blasted off into action. He landed all five quad jumps, dazzled the judges, and secured his gold medal!

Ten days later, he sat on the set of *Today*, a morning TV show. He was there with his mom. He lifted his gold medal from around his neck and placed it around his mother's neck instead. "There is no way I would be able to make it to where I am without her support," he told the interviewers. "She gave me structure . . . and made it a sport I really love."

He also added, "Even now, she continues to support me whenever I need it."

Hetty had sacrificed a lot for Nathan over the last twenty years. But when she watched him win his gold medal she said, "Inside, my heart was so happy."

Nathan returned to Yale later that year, where he looked forward to being just another college student. He was ready to make friends and focus on his studies.

When he was asked if he would keep competing, he said, "I have no idea. I'm really happy with the

44

things I have already accomplished." No matter what the future holds, Nathan has engraved his name in the figure skating record books and will forever be known as the Quad King to his fans around the world.

Timeline of Nathan Chen's Life

1999 — Nathan Chen is born on May 5 in Salt Lake City, Utah

2002 — The Winter Olympics are held in Salt Lake City, Utah

2003 — Nathan begins competing

2010 — Wins the US Championships at the novice level

2011 — Moves to California with his mom to train full-time with his coach, Rafael Arutunian

2012 — Wins the US Championships at the junior level and the ISP Junior Grand Prix in Austria

2016 — Competes at the US Championships at the senior level and places third

2017 — Skates with worn-out skates at his first World Championships and places sixth

2018 — Places fifth in the Winter Olympics

— Wins his first World Championships

— Starts college at Yale University while continuing to train

2019 — First singles skater to win all ISP Grand Prix events three years in a row

2021 — Becomes the first person to win five US Championships in a row since 1952

2022 — Wins gold medal at the Winter Olympics; also wins silver in the team event

— Returns to Yale to finish his last few years of college

Timeline of the World

1999 — The first episode of *SpongeBob SquarePants* airs on Nickelodeon

2000 — Sony launches the PlayStation 2 gaming system

2005 — Hurricane Katrina hits Louisiana and floods New Orleans as one of the deadliest and costliest storms the United States has ever seen

2006 — Nintendo Wii gaming system is released

2007 — Apple introduces the iPhone

2008 — Barack Obama elected as the first African American president of the United States

2014 — Pro-democracy protests erupt in Hong Kong and last for many months

2016 — Donald Trump is elected the forty-fifth president of the United States

2020 — A coronavirus pandemic sweeps across the world, killing millions of people; social distancing, mask wearing, and new safety protocols are created to help slow the spread of the virus

2021 — On January 6, violent protesters break into the US Capitol to stop lawmakers from certifying the lawful results of the 2020 elections; hundreds of people are injured, including 138 police officers, and five people die as a result of the attack

Bibliography

Brennan, Christine. "Nathan Chen Elevates U.S. Hopes for Figure
Skating Gold at Winter Olympics." *USA Today*, February 2,
2018.

Chen, Nathan, with Alice Park. *One Jump at a Time: My Story*.
New York: HarperCollins, 2022.

"Figure Skating—Men's Free Skating, Beijing 2022 Winter
Olympics, Full Replay." February 9, 2022. YouTube video,
4:24:04. https://www.youtube.com/watch?v=O8cvyDXX
99Y.

Hersh, Philip. "From Michelle Kwan to Nathan Chen, Passing an
Olympic Torch of Representation." **NBC Sports**, February 10,
2022.

Hersh, Philip. "Salt Lake Teenager Nathan Chen Revolutionizing Figure Skating but Trails at World Championships." *Deseret News*, March 30, 2017.

Jag, Julie. "What Does Gold Mean to an Olympian's Family? For Nathan Chen, Full Hearts and a Trip to Disneyland." *Salt Lake Tribune*, February 18, 2022.

Peed, Alicia Thompson. "Keeping Balance: Yale's Nathan Chen and the Pursuit of Olympic Gold." *Yale News*, October 25, 2021.

Rutherford, Lynn. "Young Man in a Hurry: For Nathan Chen, Actions Speak Louder—and More Often—than Words." *Skating*, November 2016.